KNOWLEDGE ENCYCLOPEDIA
BIRDS

© Wonder House Books 2024

All rights reserved. No part of this book may be reproduced or transmitted in any form by any means, electronic or mechanical, including photocopying and recording, or by any information storage and retrieval system except as may be expressly permitted in writing by the publisher.

(An imprint of Prakash Books)

contact@wonderhousebooks.com

Disclaimer: The information contained in this encyclopedia has been collated with inputs from subject experts. All information contained herein is true to the best of the Publisher's knowledge.

ISBN : 9789354402517

Table of Contents

The Incredible World of Birds	3
Birds: Then and Now	4–5
A Peek at the Birds	6–7
Of Beaks and Birds	8–9
The Eagle's Prey	10
Seagulls	11
The Filtering Flamingo	12
The Wading Stork	13
Red Robins	14
The Sparrow's Seeds	15
The Macaw's Fruit	16
The Hummingbird's Nectar	17
Colourful Feathers	18–19
Play of Pigments	20–21
The Wonder of Wings	22
The No-Fly List	23
Amazing Homes	24–25
Migrating Birds	26–27
Breeding Season	28
Knowing Birds	30
Cause and Effect	31
Word Check	32

THE INCREDIBLE WORLD OF BIRDS

Did you know that the bee hummingbird is the smallest bird in the world? It is so small that it would easily fit in the palm of your hand! Isn't that amazing?

Earth is full of diverse birds. There are about 18,000 **species** living in habitats ranging from polar ice caps to tropical rainforests, arid deserts, open seas, and mountains.

Scientifically, the entire class of birds is called 'aves'. The name is derived from the Latin word 'avis' which means birds. So, what makes aves special? It is their ability to fly with their wings (which are modified forelimbs). The feathers on the wings help a bird fly. Read on to learn more about the incredible world of birds.

▼ Birds constitute a beautiful and interesting class of animals that rule the skies

Birds: Then and Now

You might have seen pictures of dinosaurs that roamed over Earth long before our time. Did you know that scientists have found **fossils** of dinosaurs with bird-like features? This has led them to believe that dinosaurs were the ancestors of birds. It is said the ancestors of birds were theropod dinosaurs. The famous *Tyrannosaurus rex* belongs to the same family.

▶ *Dakotaraptors of the theropod family in a fight during the Late Cretaceous period. Notice the feathers on its arms, tails, and legs*

▲ *Modern birds evolved in the Jurassic and Cretaceous eras alongside dinosaurs*

The Missing Link

Have you heard about the Solnhofen Limestone? This is a geographical formation found in Germany. Its speciality is that many fossilised organisms were found here.

In 1861, a startling discovery was made here, which later came to be known as the missing link between dinosaurs and birds. A fossil of a creature named *Archaeopteryx* was found. It was first classified as a bird, but after finding fossils of similar bird-like creatures, it was reclassified as a dinosaur in the 20th century.

The *Archaeopteryx* had small teeth similar to a dinosaur and wings and feathers, similar to a bird. It lived about 147 million years ago in the Late Jurassic period. It was the size of a big hen, but with a light body that could glide through trees.

Incredible Individuals

Sir David Attenborough is a British naturalist and broadcaster. He filmed various animals in their natural environments and educated viewers on how they behave in the wild. He has received several awards for his programmes.

The Modern Birds

As time passed, toothed mouths were replaced with toothless and horn-shaped beaks. The *Confuciusornis* whose fossils were found in China, was the first bird to have this type of beak. It lived more than 100 million years ago and was about 25 centimetres in length.

Another bird-like creature called *Ichthyornis*, which lived 82–87 million years ago, was discovered to have a light skull with a beak. It resembled the modern seagull in how it had strong wings, (possibly) webbed feet, and ate fish. Nearly 66 million years ago, an asteroid hit Earth and wiped out the dinosaur species. However, the early birds, which were smaller in size, survived. This was because of their size and ability to adapt to the environmental changes of those times.

The first modern-day birds called the *Neornithes* emerged nearly 60 to 90 million years ago. In the next few million years, the number and types of birds increased. A journey that is believed to have started over 150 million years ago, culminated with trials and errors to create the beautiful birds we see today.

▲ *Fossil of Confuciusornis with a clearly marked beak*

Isn't It Amazing!

About 60 million years ago, South America was an island. This is where the terror birds roamed. One species of terror bird, called *Brontornis*, weighed up to 400 kilograms and ambushed its prey. Another, *Titanis*, could grow up to three-metres tall. With the continental drift, the North and South American landmasses joined at the Isthmus of Panama 2.8 million years ago. Climate change and competition from southward-migrating predatory mammals like wolves and sabre-toothed tigers drove these birds extinct in a few hundred thousand years.

Successful Evolution

When dinosaurs were wiped out of the planet, the mammals were still small and could not compete with the massive 'terror birds' that roamed the land. The birds around this time were so large that some even had a wingspan of 20 ft. The unnamed bird shown here is said to be the biggest bird that ever existed. They might have been the 'elephant birds' who are linked to modern ostriches.

Why were birds so successful? It is because they had the ability to fly. They could take off, successfully defending themselves from enemies. They were also able to reach farther than mammals to find food and shelter. Birds have met the trials of evolution so perfectly that Sir David Attenborough, a popular broadcaster and historian believes them to be the most successful creatures on Earth!

▲ *These scary birds disappeared around 2.5 million years ago*

◀ *Terror birds reached nightmarish proportions, and usually ranged from one-three metres in height and 350–400 kilograms of weight*

A Peek at the Birds

Have you ever observed birds closely? Can you think of all the different parts that give them the incredible ability to fly? Let's find out about all the important parts of a bird's body.

▼ *Macaws are the largest type of parrots*

Warm-blooded

Birds, like mammals, are warm-blooded in nature. Their bodies maintain a steady temperature regardless of the temperature of their surroundings. They do not rely on sunshine to increase heat within them during winter, or on shade to decrease the heat during summer. Usually, their bodies maintain a temperature of 40° C.

◄ *The blue and yellow macaw is found in the rain forest in South America*

Aerodynamics

Birds' bodies are adapted to fly. Their bones are light and hollow. Their legs are held close to their bodies, giving them an **aerodynamic** advantage. Birds have no external ears. This feature streamlines their bodies, allowing them to fly with very little resistance. Also, importantly, birds do not sweat as they lack sweat glands. This keeps their feathers light and dry.

▲ *An owl's eyes are adapted to seeing in the night*

In Real Life

The next time you visit a zoo, pay close attention to the owls. Observe their eyes when they blink because they appear to have a third eyelid. This is nothing but a transparent membrane that moves across the eye in most birds. It is called the nictitating membrane. It protects the eyes from injury.

Bird's-eye View

Birds have keen vision, especially birds of prey such as hawks, eagles, vultures, etc. Their eyes help them spot food from great distances. Birds of prey such as the eagle can see as far as two kilometres. Their eyes face forward, which helps them determine the distance between themselves and the prey. Birds that are preyed upon such as sparrows or pigeons—have wider and better fields of vision, as their eyes are on the side.

▶ Beaks are special to birds and they come in various sizes and shapes depending on the food they consume

Beaks and Bills

Birds have no teeth or jaws, but they have beaks, also known as bills. Beaks are primarily used to catch and eat food. They are also used to drink water, feed the young, gather materials to build nests, and for both offence and defence.

Bird Sounds

Can you imitate the sound that a crow or a peacock makes? Birds make different, often melodious, sounds. They make calls, which are short tunes. Or they may sing in long, repeated patterns.

Birds call out when they sense danger from a predator or when they are angry, worried, or guarding their territory. They also sing when they are happy or looking for a mate.

◀ The orange-bellied flowerpecker has very light feet which help it to hold onto branches of trees

Adaptations

Birds have feet which are adapted to where and how they live. A hen has feet suited to scratching the ground to find insects and seeds to eat. Commonly seen birds like pigeons, sparrows, and crows have thin feet with three toes facing frontwards and one backwards.

These types of feet help the bird perch and hold onto tree branches tightly. On the other hand, birds of prey like the eagle or vulture have strong feet with curved talons to kill the prey.

🏅 Incredible Individuals

The study of birds is enhanced by artists like John James Audubon (1785–1851) who, in his lifetime, painted a large number of birds existing in North America. He published a book titled *Birds of America* which had seven volumes.

Of Beaks and Birds

Birds use their beaks in many ways. They collect grains to feed their young and gather materials to build a nest, attack and defend, attract their mates, scratch themselves, and also use the beaks for grooming. Beaks can be classified according to size and shape as they help birds follow a specific diet.

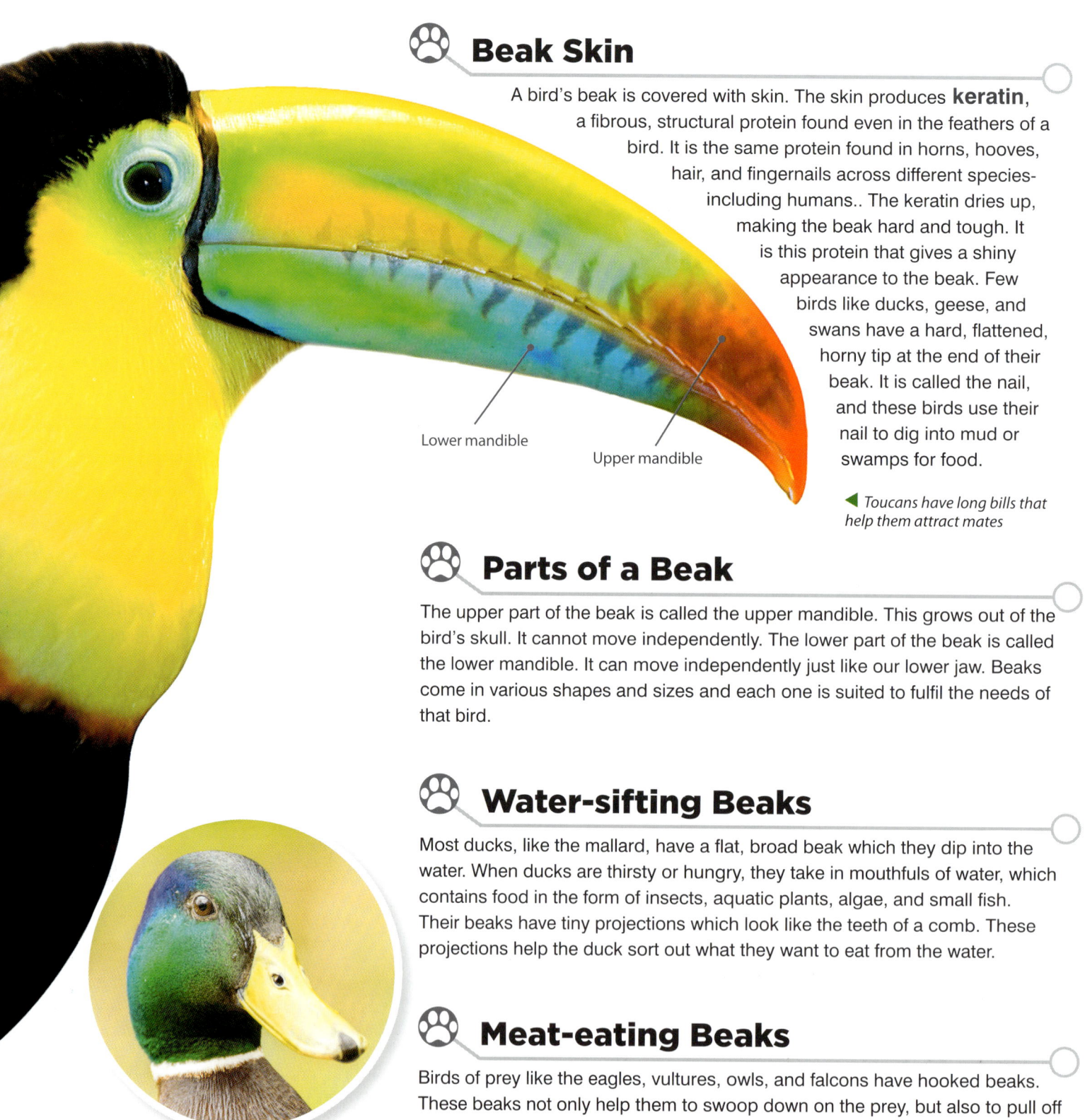

Lower mandible • Upper mandible

◀ Toucans have long bills that help them attract mates

▲ Ducks have big bills, which is a name for more fleshy beaks

Beak Skin

A bird's beak is covered with skin. The skin produces **keratin**, a fibrous, structural protein found even in the feathers of a bird. It is the same protein found in horns, hooves, hair, and fingernails across different species- including humans.. The keratin dries up, making the beak hard and tough. It is this protein that gives a shiny appearance to the beak. Few birds like ducks, geese, and swans have a hard, flattened, horny tip at the end of their beak. It is called the nail, and these birds use their nail to dig into mud or swamps for food.

Parts of a Beak

The upper part of the beak is called the upper mandible. This grows out of the bird's skull. It cannot move independently. The lower part of the beak is called the lower mandible. It can move independently just like our lower jaw. Beaks come in various shapes and sizes and each one is suited to fulfil the needs of that bird.

Water-sifting Beaks

Most ducks, like the mallard, have a flat, broad beak which they dip into the water. When ducks are thirsty or hungry, they take in mouthfuls of water, which contains food in the form of insects, aquatic plants, algae, and small fish. Their beaks have tiny projections which look like the teeth of a comb. These projections help the duck sort out what they want to eat from the water.

Meat-eating Beaks

Birds of prey like the eagles, vultures, owls, and falcons have hooked beaks. These beaks not only help them to swoop down on the prey, but also to pull off the skin, fur, or feathers of the prey; and to tear apart the meat into small bites which they can swallow.

Nectar-feeding Beaks

Hummingbirds have long, thin, needle-like beaks which they use to suck nectar from flowers. The beak is a protective covering for the tongue inside the mouth. It is this tongue that is used by the hummingbird to pull out nectar from the flowers.

▶ A pouch-like beak helps capture food better

▶ Different hummingbirds have beaks of varied size. The sword-billed hummingbird's beak can go up to 10.2 centimetres, which is longer than its body if you exclude the tail!

Fish-eating Beaks

The pelican has a huge beak with a throat pouch. The bird takes in the fish along with water into the pouch. The water is drained out and the fish is swallowed. The upper mandible in the pelican's beak has a small hook-like structure. This is used to spear the fish.

Fruit-and-nut-eating Beaks

Birds that eat fruits and nuts, such as parrots or macaws, have smaller beaks with hooked tips. These tips are used to rip off the skin of fruits and reach the fleshy and sweet interior. These birds also use their beaks to break tough nuts down to edible pieces.

▲ Parrots are often called 'hookbills', based on the shape of their beak/bill

Seed-eating Birds

Seed-eating birds use their short beaks to pick up seeds to eat. Sparrows, like most such birds, have cone-shaped beaks that they use to peck on seeds.

▶ The Gouldian finch is a seed eater

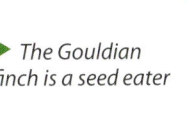

◀ A beak with a hook gives a good grip to catch prey

👤 In Real Life

Birds use their beaks to feed their young. An eagle captures prey and breaks it into small chunks. The eaglet (as its baby is called) snatches the feed from its parent and swallows it. Most eaglets eat one to eight times a day.

▲ The baby bird that screeches louder than others usually gets more food

The Eagle's Prey

A large beak, two heavy talons, and a keen stare—these are the features that distinguish eagles from all other birds. Of the eagles, there are two distinct species that we can see around North America. These are the bald eagle and the golden eagle.

Bald v/s Golden

The bald eagle gets its name from the old English word 'balde' which means 'white'. It refers to the cover of snowy-white feathers on the bald eagle's head. This proud bird is the national symbol of the USA. On the other hand, the golden eagle is the national bird of Mexico. It is the largest bird of prey in North America. It gets its name from the cover of golden-brown feathers on its head.

▶ The golden eagle can grow to a length of 3 ft, with a wingspan of 6-7 ft

▲ The bald eagle approaching a perch to rest upon. This is also how they look when they are ready to snatch a rabbit from the ground

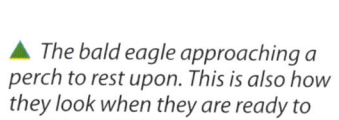 On the Hunt

Along with buzzards, kites, vultures, harriers, and hawks, eagles are called birds of prey. They follow a carnivorous diet and hunt their food. Eagles can be found in many areas, but they like to live in really high places from where they watch for movement on the land below. All birds of prey have a sharp, hooked curve at the end of their beaks. The upper part of the beak extends over the lower. They also have curved and pointed claws called talons.

Once they spot a prey, such as a fish in the water or a little rabbit burrowing in the ground, they swoop down quickly to catch it with their sharp talons. Eagles feed on reptiles, smaller birds, and **carrion**. Sometimes, they might attack a large deer or even steal meat from other animals.

▶ An eagle's grip is up to 10 times stronger than that of humans"

In Real Life

A popular myth says that Ben Franklin wasn't keen on the nomination of the bald eagle as the national symbol of USA because he had learned that eagles like to steal the kills of other animals. However, eagles have long been seen as a symbol of strength, war, and absolute power since the Babylonian era.

Seagulls

There are more than 40 species of gulls. You can distinguish between them by looking at the spots of colour on their legs and beaks. For example, the herring gull has a red spot on the lower part of its beak. Gulls have strong and gently hooked beaks. They use these to catch and hold fish and water from the sea.

▲ Seagulls can use breadcrumbs to attract fish

Diet

Gulls are **piscivorous** birds, which means they primarily eat fish. They also enjoy molluscs, worms, insects, and crustaceans. They mainly find food on beaches, but in heavily populated areas they might sift through garbage bins looking for food.

Bigger or older seagulls are so bold that they steal the eggs laid by other birds. The herring gull is known for being a thief. It is seen stealing food from beachgoers and other gulls. It might look for rabbits and even wait patiently for them to peep out of their burrows.

Dropped Meals

Gulls enjoy molluscs and crustaceans, but they have hard shells. So, how do the birds eat them? Cleverly, the gulls carry these molluscs in their beaks as they fly and drop them from a height onto hard rocks so that their shells crack.

▲ A gull's intelligence is clearly demonstrated in the way they eat molluscs. They drop them from heights to crack the shell and get to the soft insides

Intelligent Behaviour

Gulls are highly intelligent birds. The black-headed gulls practice an interesting method called 'eggshell removal'. After their eggs hatch, these gulls rush to move the eggshells far away from the newly hatched chicks. This practice protects the chicks from getting injured by the sharp edges of the broken eggshells.

This removal also prevents predators like the herring gulls and crows from preying on the chicks. The insides of the eggs, which have certain odours, attract these predators. When these eggshells are moved away, the predators fly towards the eggshells, leaving the chicks safe.

Incredible Individuals

> Nikolaas Tinbergen (1907–1988) was a British zoologist who studied the behaviour of the black-headed gulls. He wanted to know why they carried eggshells away from their chicks, so he carried out an experiment where he left one set of eggs out in the open and another set of false eggs with eggshells. He noticed that crows went to the decoy eggs rather than the real ones because of the presence of the eggshells.

▲ Some studies show that if you stare them down, seagulls will hesitate a little longer before grabbing your French fry

The Filtering Flamingo

A group of flamingos is called a flock or flamboyance. If you live in South America, Africa, or certain parts of Europe and Asia, you have probably seen these flamboyant birds. They have long, slender, and curved necks and wide, flat black-tipped beaks. The pink feathers that cover their bodies are their most unique feature.

▲ Flamingos flock together in thousands near water bodies where they can filter-feed for shrimp, algae, and insects

Social Habits

It is rare to see a flamingo on its own, as it is an extremely social bird. They are seen in groups of hundreds or even millions near lakes. They keep themselves warm by standing on one leg, keeping the raised leg dry. These birds build their nests out of the mud available on the shores. They stack up the mud in the shape of a cone until it stands several inches above the ground. It is here that they lay their eggs.

Diet

Flamingos feed by bending their long necks down and pushing their beaks underwater. They disturb the ground beneath the water by moving their feet, shuffling the organic matter about. This ruffles up delicious servings of plankton, algae, small fish, larvae, and mini-invertebrates such as crustaceans and molluscs.

Unfortunately, they also catch some muddy water in their beaks along with the food. So, they simply move their heads side-to-side to filter out the water. Their short beaks have small structures within, which help this process along. Then, they simply expel the water from their beaks. Ducks and swans also possess this filtering ability.

▲ Male and female flamingos build a nest together and both sit on the egg while it incubates for about a month

In Real Life

The flashy pink colour of the flamingos' feathers comes from their diet. Baby flamingos are born with a white or grey plumage that only turns pink after two years of eating food that contains carotenoid pigments. Flamingos in zoos consume food colouring so that this pink colour does not fade.

▲ The feathers under flamingos' wings are black

◀ The flamingo is the national bird of The Bahamas

ANIMALS | BIRDS

The Wading Stork

In many countries, children are told that they were delivered to their parents by the stork. The image is always of a stork with its almost-straight beak carrying a baby wrapped within a blanket. In reality, storks use their long beaks to fish for food and communicate by making a bill-clattering noise that sounds like distant machine-gun fire.

▼ The myth can be traced back to Greek roots, where Hera changed one of Zeus's lovers into a stork as revenge

Fishing Time

Storks prefer to feed during the day and like to catch fish and other small animals. Some only eat carrion. When storks feel hungry, they fly above water with their beaks open. They put their beaks in the water and appear to walk above the surface. As soon as a fish gets close to the beak, the storks close it. They take as little as 25 milliseconds to do this, so the poor trapped fish cannot escape. As a result of this remarkable feeding habit, storks are called wading birds. They are seen moving and even standing still in the water. The spoonbill is another example of a wading bird.

Storks usually wade above freshwater lakes and ponds where there are plenty of fish. They are seen in the warmer areas of Asia, Africa, and Europe. They like to feed in flocks as they love being around other storks. During the breeding season they break into pairs—each pair happily eating around 180 kilograms of fish in one season.

▲ A stork approaching the water to begin feeding

▲ Black storks sometimes kill their weak babies when there is shortage of food

Isn't It Amazing!

Storks do not have a vocal organ or 'syrinx', so they do not have a call like most other birds. Instead, if they want to make a sound, they clatter their beaks in different ways to share a feeling of excitement.

Incredible Individuals

India and Cambodia have seen a decline in their number of storks due to deforestation. Unhappy with this development, a group of 70 women from Assam, India formed the Hargilla Army. (Hargilla is the name given to storks in Sanskrit.)

Storks build nesting trees which were lost after deforestation. They also suffered from the poor impression they made on the locals because of their smell and large size. So, the Hargilla Army educated people about the importance of storks and protecting the trees, making sure that no more nesting trees were cut down since 2010.

▲ Storks are known to stay and continue breeding in one nest for many years

Red Robins

There are two main species of robins; they are the American robin and the European robin. The American robin is bigger, with a length of 25 centimetres while the European robin is around 10 centimetres. They can be distinguished by the colour of the feathers on their breast—rusty red if American, and scarlet orange if European.

◀ American robin is the state bird for Connecticut, Michigan, and Wisconsin

▶ European robin can cope with cold and snow, but far northern Europe can still be too much

Diet

American robins prefer to feed on a diet of small insects, earthworms, and delicious berries. European robins mainly eat insects like grasshoppers and caterpillars. Both species like to look for food during the day. European robins live in suburban areas and follow gardeners. As the gardener goes about digging the ground, the robin quickly grabs any insect that might be disturbed from the soil. Similarly, American robins spend most of their day hopping around on grass, looking for earthworms.

Feeding Habits

Robins have thin, straight beaks that are quite small. Other insect-eating birds like swallows might fly close to the ground with their beaks apart, ready to catch an insect whether it is stationary or moving. On the other hand, robins prefer to catch insects while standing in one place. They practice a run-and-stop technique to catch their food. Robins also rest on the branches of trees and pluck berries individually with their beaks.

▲ If there is a choice of foods, most robins prefer meal worms above other things

The Songbird

Robins, like sparrows, live in populated areas and do not mind the presence of human beings. They have sweet, melodious voices, and they sing to other birds to communicate and mate. The European robin tends to emit high-pitched notes throughout the year. The American robins sing before and after sunrise. They only repeat two or three 'syllables' when they sing but it is cheery and pleasant to hear.

▼ Each robin has a unique breast pattern and can be recognised individually

▶ Both male and female robins sing the same winter song

The Sparrow's Seeds

Sparrows are such a common sight, they seem like the most common bird in the world. One of their species, the house sparrows, are the most widely seen in the world. These birds, along with goldfinches, are seed- and grain-eating birds.

House Sparrows

House sparrows, like all other sparrows, have short and cone-shaped beaks. They use these to break the seeds and eat them. Their legs are short. Though they are small and just around 15 centimetres in length, these birds have stout bodies. They are often on the lookout for any crumbs of food they can find. They might even steal from other birds like the American robin.

▶ House sparrows just weigh around 30 grams

Lark Sparrows

Lark sparrows like to roam along sandy or barren lands to find seeds or grains. They are about the same size as the house sparrow. As soon as they feel too warm or sense a threat, they find a tall perch to sit on. These birds avoid confrontation. They might fly away in a hurry if they are approached by human beings.

▶ The harlequin facial pattern and white tail spots make the lark sparrow standout among sparrows

Golden-Crowned Sparrows

The golden-crowned sparrows get their name from the small patch of yellow plumage visible at the top of their crown or head. During the winter season, these sparrows join the flock of the other sparrow species for protection. These birds eat seeds from fruits and flowers in open garden areas. They also happily nip at vegetables like peas, beets, and cabbages.

Golden-crowned sparrows can be seen in the fall and spring seasons in shrubs and weeds. The birds use their beaks to scratch leaves or peck on them to find seeds. They are often spotted hopping on the ground.

Fox Sparrows

Fox sparrows are seen in places where there is thick shrubbery or plant cover. They like to eat small seeds that they might find on the ground. They also eat small berries. They might be seen scratching up bird feeders that people have left out. These sparrows are named for their reddish plumage. However, while some birds have the fox-like red covering, other birds might display a dark brown or even grey cover of feathers.

▶ The call of a golden-crowned sparrow sounds like a whistle

▶ Fox sparrows spend a lot of time on the ground

The Macaw's Fruit

Macaws belong to the parrot family. There are 18 different species found in North and South America. A unique thing about macaws is that despite being a colourful species, both the male and female look like each other.

Beaks and Skills

Macaws have curved, sickle-shaped beaks where the upper part of the beak extends over the lower. These beaks are big enough to hold nuts in, and strong enough to crack them apart with little effort. The macaws also have strong, muscly tongues with a strong bone that helps them break into the juicy insides of a fruit. After they crack open a nut, they tap at the insides with their tongues.

◀ *A macaw grips the fruit with its toes*

Interestingly, they also use their tongues and beaks to explore their surroundings. They grip tree branches with their toes and also use these toes to reach for and grab fruits and nuts.

Diet

Macaws climb trees and look for fruits, nuts, flowers, and leaves. They enjoy the pulp and seeds of fruits. Some species gather at riverbanks to eat the clayey soil. They also lick at the clay on the riverbanks as it has a lot of sodium. This helps them detoxify their bodies. Along with the macaws, the parakeets, parrots, and cockatoos are also frugivorous birds.

◀ *The great green macaws are 85-90 centimetres long*

Notable Macaws

The hyacinth macaw is the largest parrot and is found in Brazil, Paraguay, and Bolivia. It has a length of 100 centimetres on an average. The scarlet macaw is most famous among macaws. While the hyacinth macaw has a cobalt-blue plumage, the scarlet macaw has yellow, blue, and red plumage. Its white head easily displays that it is excited and blushing. Though they have a reputation for being difficult, macaws are still kept as pets by people around the world.

▶ *Macaws typically pick a partner and stay with them for life*

In Real Life

It is not easy to keep macaws as pets. Acquiring them can be difficult and expensive. They might make many angry noises and yelps or shrieks. They might also gnaw on a person's fingers and even bite them with their strong beaks. However, if cared for properly, they can live for as long as 100 years.

▶ *Hyacinth macaws can live up to 80 years*

The Hummingbird's Nectar

It is not just bees that hover near flowers for nectar. They get plenty of competition from birds who feed on nectar. These birds usually have thin, long beaks that they can push into the inside of a flower. One such example is the hummingbird.

▲ Hummingbirds are the only birds than can hover in place. They do this by flapping their wings 20-80 times a second, and can move in any direction

 ## Pollination and Diet

Hummingbirds repeatedly and quickly move their wings so that they can hover in mid-air. This way they use their beaks to feed on the sap, flowers, and nectar in the plants that they hover near. As they feed on nectar, they move from flower to flower and pollinate them. For some flowers, they might be the only source of pollination.

Hummingbirds might also feed on insects and spiders as they need to eat about two times their body weight in food. They need to do this to have enough energy to rapidly beat their wings. The rapid beating of their wings leads to a hum, which is why these birds are called hummingbirds.

▲ The violet sabrewing is the largest species of hummingbird in Middle America

Isn't It Amazing!

Usually, there are one or two collective nouns used for a group of animals. The hummingbird is unique as there are many collective nouns used to describe a group of these beautiful birds. You can call them a 'hover', 'shimmer', 'tune', or even 'bouquet'. Commonly, a group of hummingbirds is called a 'charm'. In the Caribbean, people call the hummingbird 'el zunzun'.

Incredible Individuals

John Gould (1804–1881) was a British ornithologist who named several species of hummingbirds based on their exotic appearances. He called them names like sun, sapphire, wood star, fairy, and coquette according to the colour of their feathers.

 ## Anna's Hummingbird

The Anna's hummingbirds are unusual in that their normal body temperature is around 41° C. If their surrounding temperature falls, these hummingbirds experience a slower heart rate and as a result, their body temperature drops to nearly 8° C. They become active again once they reach their normal body temperature.

▲ Anna's hummingbird was named after Anna Masséna, the Duchess of Rivoli

Colourful Feathers

A unique feature of birds is their ability to fly. It is enabled by feathers and wings. Most birds have bright and colourful feathers with striking patterns. Besides flying, they use their feathers to keep warm in winters, keep cool in summers, camouflage themselves from predators, and attract mates.

Inside Feathers

Feathers are made of a fibrous structural protein called keratin. Each feather consists of a hollow shaft and two vanes or two halves on either side. The vanes are made up of hundreds of thin branch-like barbs. On both sides of each barb, there could be still smaller branches called barbules.

▲ *The flight feathers of the hawk help it take turns while catching prey*

A Variety of Feathers

Feathers are roughly divided into six types—contour, flight, down, filoplume, semiplume, and bristle.

Contour

Contour feathers are those which cover the entire body surface and give a smooth and colourful appearance. They are waterproof and protect the bird from heavy wind and hot temperatures. These contour feathers provide the streamlined structure that allows birds to fly. Contour feathers can be seen on the wings and tail of the bird where they grow from follicles present on the bird's skin.

▶ *This bird has contour feathers on its tail and its wings. These feathers give it a streamlined shape*

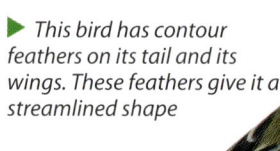

Hollow shaft

Vane

Afterfeather

In Real Life

Nearly once every year, a bird will shed its contour feathers. These feathers will be replaced eventually. The process takes place after the breeding season is over. Even before the breeding season begins, some birds will shed some part of their contour feathers, which will then be replaced. This usually happens during the first winter of the season. This process is called '**moulting**' in birds.

▶ *Adult robins moult at the end of the mating season*

02 Flight

Flight feathers are found in the wings and tails of birds. Of these, the flight feathers near the birds' bodies are called tertiaries. The flight feathers at the tail end are called retrices. Normally, birds have 12 tail feathers that they use to stop or make turns during flight. At the base of all flight feathers there are much smaller contour feathers called coverts which cover the wings and ears.

Rachis • Barb

03 Down

Down feathers are under the contour ones and keep the birds insulated. When chicks are born, they are covered with down feathers to keep warm, but as they grow and get ready for the world, these are replaced by contour feathers to aid flight.

▼ Down feathers have a fluffy appearance as their barbs are not joined together

04 Filoplume

Filoplumes are the long, thin, and hair-like feathers with few barbs at the ends. Their function is still under debate, but they are thought to be sensory in nature. Some scientists believe that they help adjust the position of other feathers in response to air pressure.

05 Semiplume

The semiplumes shape and insulate the bird and are also useful for aerodynamics. They have long shafts and downy tips.

06 Bristle

Bristle feathers protect the birds but also act as their sensory organs. These might not be present in all birds. An insect-eating bird might have bristle feathers near the head or neck.

Bristle feathers are present near the eyelids and beak. They might be funnels that aid insect-eating birds in catching their food. These birds need to scoop insects from the earth, which bristle feathers help them do. Woodpeckers, for example, have bristle feathers near their nostrils where they act as a filter to aid the bird while it pecks at a tree.

▶ Many insect-eating birds need bristle feathers for feeding

Shed Me!

Birds shed feathers and replace them with new ones. This process is called moulting. It helps keep the feathers in good condition as it replaces the damaged and worn-out ones. Moulting is a time- and energy-consuming process. Hence, birds usually moult when they are not nesting or migrating.

How regularly do birds moult? Do they shed all their feathers at once? Some birds like eagles moult gradually and over a period of time so that they do not lose all their feathers at a time, and are capable of flying. On the other hand, birds like ducks lose their flight feathers immediately after the nesting season. During the few weeks it takes for the feathers to grow back, they remain flightless. But they do not go hungry since they find food by walking or swimming.

Isn't It Amazing!

Can you imagine rubbing ants all over your body? It would hurt your skin! But birds like crows like to go 'anting' during moulting. It means to pick up ants with their beaks and rub them on their feathers and skin. The birds may also lie near anthills to allow the insects to crawl all over them. They do this because secretions from the ants soothe their irritated skin during moulting.

Play of Pigments

Feathers get their colours either due to pigments or because of light refraction caused due to the shape of the feather. Pigments are naturally colouring substances in plants, birds, and animals. In birds, pigments come in three varieties called melanin, carotenoids, and porphyrins.

Melanin

Melanin is found in both the skin and feathers of a bird. It produces colours such as black, brown, and yellow. Melanin is also known to make feathers strong and resistant. It is the primary pigment in birds such as crows, owls, and hawks.

◀ *Birds use colours to identify others of their species.*

▲ *Flamingos are born with grey feathers that slowly turn pink because of carotenoids*

Carotenoids

Birds cannot produce carotenoids but they acquire them from the food they eat. These pigments produce colours such as bright red, orange, and yellow. The flamingo looks pink, but it will lose its colour if it does not eat carotenoid-rich foods like shrimp and algae. Goldfinches and cardinals also need carotenoids.

Researchers say that there might be benefits to human consumption of carotenoids. It might reduce the risk of eye diseases and even some types of cancers. Beta-carotene is a carotenoid that is found in carrots. It can be converted into vitamin A which is beneficial for the eyes. Some carotenoids even absorb blue light that enters the eye from screens of the gadgets that we use.

In Real Life

Have you seen a bird preening? It refers to the process of cleaning and tidying the feathers. A bird preens to make sure the feathers work properly. For this, it squeezes out oil from the oil gland under its tail. With the help of the beak and claws it rubs this oil along the length of the feathers. The feathers become shiny, smooth, and waterproof.

▲ *When resting, birds may preen at least once an hour*

ANIMALS | BIRDS

Porphyrins

Porphyrins are pigments that can produce pink, green, and brown colours in birds. Some species of hummingbirds and peacocks get their shimmering colours from this pigment and the structure of their feathers. The colours are produced because of light refracted by the protein in the feather. The colours might vary depending on the angle at which the feather is viewed.

◀ *The Guinea turaco has a green plumage because of porphyrins*

Hide Me, See Me

Camouflage is used to conceal or blend oneself with the surroundings for safety. Birds camouflage to protect themselves as well as their eggs and later the young ones from predators. Colourful feathers are the best tools for disguise; the white-tailed ptarmigan is a great example of the same. In winter, the feathers of this bird—that resides in high altitudes—turn snow-white to blend in with the snow. In summer, the bird is streaked grey and brown. However, its tail remains white throughout the year.

▲ *A white-tailed ptarmigan is also referred to as snow quail*

Attracting a Mate

Birds also use their feathers to attract mates, as done by the peacocks. During mating season, the male peacock spreads out its beautiful blue and green tail and puts on an elaborate show to attract the peahen, a regular-looking, brown bird. Flamingos, the beautiful pink birds, rub themselves with carotenoid-rich oil from their tail glands to look pinker and more desirable to their mates.

▼ *Peacocks take three years to grow their tail feathers*

The Wonder of Wings

▲ The huge wings of eagles help them soar and glide with minimal effort

Do you ever wonder how or why wings evolved? One theory states that forelimbs were modified into wings. According to another theory, wings were used as display objects to attract mates, while still another says wings evolved from gliding ancestors. Whichever the theory, birds could not have taken flight without these structures.

Is it a Bird? Is it a Plane?

The wings of an aeroplane are modelled on bird wings. Wings are attached to powerful chest muscles. They are convex on the upper surface, concave on the lower, and they taper from front to back.

When a bird flies, air flows at greater speed at the upper part of the wing than the lower part because of its shape, creating less pressure on the top. This helps lift the bird during flight.

How Birds Use Wings

There are different types of wings based on the flight of the bird. Birds of prey like eagles, vultures, and hawks have soaring wings that are large and broad. The moment the bird spots prey, it closes its wings and dives down, opening them again to slow down as it nears the ground to make a soft landing.

◄ A Cape vulture has a wingspan of 2.26–2.6 metres

► Adult European gulls have white heads and bodies and grey wings

Birds such as seagulls and Arctic terns have gliding wings. These are long, narrow, and flat, with no space between the feathers. Gliding wings allow the birds to fly without having to spend much energy to stay in the air. Gliding refers to a bird moving in a downward direction closer to land and thus it must occasionally flap its wings to regain height.

◄ The flying sparrow has high-speed wings

Small birds such as house sparrows, woodpeckers, and thrushes must be quick to escape their predators. They have elliptical wings. These rapid take-off wings have spaces between the feathers, making them lighter and easier to move. These wings are not made for sustained flight and the birds must expend a lot of energy to stay airborne for long periods of time. Scavenger birds such as crows and ravens also have elliptical wings that help them steal food and escape quickly.

Birds such as swallows and swifts, which must catch their food mid-air at times, have high-speed wings. These wings are long, narrow, and pointed. They are angled backwards, making rapid flight easy.

ANIMALS | BIRDS

The No-Fly List

It is not true that all birds fly. Even though they have wings, birds like ostriches, emus, kiwis, rheas, and cassowaries cannot fly. Their flat breastbone, to which the strong flight muscles are attached, lack a keel. This means that their wings are weak and cannot take off the ground. Flightless birds as a group are called **ratites**.

Long Lost Cousins

It is believed that ratites are related to a group of 47 South American birds called 'tinamou'. While ratites lost their ability to fly over time, tinamous are capable of flight, but prefer to walk on the ground.

Scientists believe that over millions of years, ratites lost flight as a trait as they adapted to their environment. Wings became a redundant feature. However, the birds evolved strong muscular legs instead, making them fast runners and offering an alternative way to escape predators.

World's Biggest Bird

The ostrich is the largest living flightless bird. It is native to the continent of Africa. In fact, even the egg the ostrich lays is the largest of all eggs, each about 6 inches in length, 15-18 inches in circumference, and around 1.4 kilograms. When it senses danger, the bird shoots off at a speed of 72 kmph and while facing a threat, it is known to kick hard.

The Australian Wonder

The emu is the second-largest living bird in the world. It is about 5 feet tall and is found on the continent of Australia. Like the ostrich it runs very fast, at 48 kmph, and kicks at the predator.

South American Rhea

Rheas are found in South America. They are omnivores, which means that they eat both plants and animals. They are related to the ostrich and emu—who live in different continents. But, they are much smaller, measuring 4 feet in height and 20 kilograms in weight.

Rheas are of two types—the common rhea which is found in Brazil and Argentina, and its cousin, which is a slightly smaller bird called Darwin's rhea, which lives in areas starting from Peru, all the way down to Patagonia.

💡 Isn't It Amazing!

When dinosaurs were wiped off the planet, mammals were still small and had not yet evolved to become apex predators. Instead, birds underwent what is known as an 'evolutionary explosion'—occupying several ecological niches. Some, like the hummingbird, evolved to be very tiny and live on nectar, while others like the giant moa became large herbivores. Birds were successful because they could fly and take off at will, successfully defending themselves from enemies. They were also able to reach farther than mammals to find food and shelter.

◀ The adult ostrich is 9 ft in height

▶ Emus are the only birds with calf muscles

◀ Ostriches have two toes, but rheas have three

▼ One ostrich egg is equivalent to 24 hen's eggs

Amazing Homes

Birds build nests to lay eggs and nurture their young ones. It is a tedious task because they have no workforce, cement, bricks, and tiles. They use their beaks and feet to put a home together with basic material such as grass, twigs, leaves, mud, stones, and even small pieces of cloth. Some birds do not build nests; they dig small, shallow holes to lay eggs, while others lay eggs on open land.

Sociable Weaver
The sociable weaver bird is a species found in South Africa. These birds believe in community living. They build huge nests with individual chambers which can house more than 100 breeding pairs of birds. Nests are built with grass and can reach a height of 3 metres. One can find these nests perched on trees and poles.

Hammerhead
It is a wading bird found in Africa and Madagascar. It builds 4–5 nests a year using as many as 10,000 pieces of twigs, reeds, and grasses. It holds the nest together with mud as this provides insulation on cold nights. Both male and female birds build nests that can span 4 feet in height and weigh up to 50 kilograms.

European Bee-eater
The European bee-eater is a small bird found in southern Europe and parts of Africa and Asia. The bird nests in a hole in the riverbanks sand. It drills the hole with its beak and then clears the sand with its feet, making a small burrow. It is a smart bird, as it makes sure the soil is soft enough to drill a hole, but also safe enough to prevent caving in.

Swiftlet

The swiftlet is a small bird dwelling in South East Asia. The unique thing about this bird is that it builds its nest with its own saliva. The nest is built in layers, usually on walls of caves, buildings, or against cliffs. The birds live in huge colonies. The nest is used in a delicacy called the bird's-nest soup in Chinese cuisine.

Common Murres

The common murres are medium-sized water birds. These are commonly seen on the Pacific Coast in places such as Alaska and Canada, near bays and the ocean. These birds nest on open ledges on rock cliffs. Their nests are huge, packed colonies. Since the eggs are in the open, one of the parents stands guard to protect it from predators.

Cuckoo

Cuckoos do not build their own nests, instead, they let other birds do all the work. They lay eggs in magpie nests. Instead of waiting for the magpies to leave the nest, research has shown that female cuckoos force the female magpies out of the nest to lay their eggs. Some cuckoo birds resemble the predatory hawk, scaring the magpie into fleeing, while the cuckoo reaches the nest without a fight. The poor female magpie then incubates these eggs along with her own.

Flamingo

Flamingos live in colonies. During the breeding season, most of these birds mate at the same time, laying eggs in smooth conical mud piles, which are their nests. The nests are built by both males and females in shallow lagoons.

Bald Eagle

Bald eagles build nests (called eyries) high up on tree branches from where they can view their surroundings and others cannot reach easily. The nest is usually close to water. Both male and female eagles build the nest with small branches, grass, and twigs. They are not just deep, but large as well, and can span as much as 5 feet wide.

Migrating Birds

Migration is a periodic, seasonal movement of animals from one place to another. It is particularly evident in birds. Most often, birds leave a place in autumn and return to it in spring. To avoid harsh winters they move to a place with plenty of sunshine and food. Migration and breeding are both required for survival of the different species of birds.

🐾 Path Taken

Migrating birds take the same route every year and usually it is the direct path between two places. This is done to conserve energy. It is said that for navigation they depend on the movement of the Sun and Earth's magnetic field. Hills, mountains, forests, rivers and coastlines act as guides during the trip.

Some species of birds use the night skies to fly to their destination. The orientation of the stars helps them steer in the right direction. Birds usually migrate in flocks and many use the V-shaped formation while flying to conserve their energy.

 About 40 per cent of birds all over the world migrate regularly

 Robins are fiercely territorial over food supply

🐾 A Dangerous Journey

During migration, birds face many hazards in the form of storms, predators, and at times disorientation, especially while crossing deserts or large water bodies like seas and oceans. Added to this list are the dangers they face from human activity like habitat loss because of deforestation, skyscrapers, cell phone towers, television towers, and electric cables.

🐾 Little Birdies

Apart from survival, birds have another purpose for migration. In spring, when the weather is good, there is plenty of food and foliage to hide their eggs and keep young ones safe. Birds return to their breeding grounds to procreate. However, there is one bird which returns to its nesting ground in winter to lay eggs. It is the emperor penguin!

 Emperor penguins are the tallest and heaviest of all penguin species

In Real Life

Siberian cranes are an **endangered species**. Every year, the birds migrate from their habitats in Central Asia to reach India during the winter season. However, in the past few years, none of these migrating birds have been spotted in India, especially in Bharatpur, Rajasthan, which was famous for their sightings. This might be due to ecological damage to their habitat and hunting of these beautiful birds for their meat.

▲ Siberian cranes feed on roots and berries

▲ Red grouse are ground-dwelling birds, but they can also fly short distances and perform twists and turns in the air

◄ Migratory route of the Arctic tern. They have the longest annual migration of any animal on Earth

▲ Arctic terns migrate to and from the Arctic Circle and the Antarctic Circle

Arctic Tern

This small bird breeds in summer in the Arctic. In the autumn it is ready to fly south to Antarctica. After spending about three months there, it flies back once more to Greenland or Canada where it dwells. The bird is special because it travels the longest migratory distance of any animal on this planet. It covers a total of about 96,000 kilometres in a roundabout trip.

Sedentary Birds

Some birds like the Siberian crane and Eurasian cuckoo are known to migrate thousands of kilometres, while others such as the American robin travel short distances. Some birds like the red grouse found in Great Britain do not migrate at all. Such birds are called sedentary or resident birds.

Sedentary birds do not migrate because they find food all year long in places where they reside. Few birds such as the skylarks and snow buntings migrate from their homes in higher altitudes to lower altitudes in winters.

Isn't It Amazing!

Lesser flamingos live in the Rift Valley of Africa and feed on algal blooms found in the lakes in the area. These blooms could be toxic to many, but lesser flamingos thrive on them. The interesting fact is that the birds are not migratory, but nomadic, moving from one lake to another in search of ample food.

▲ Flamingos can filter feed in water for several hours a day

Breeding Season

For the emperor penguin, the breeding season usually starts in April. This is autumn in Antarctica. The sea ice, which might have melted in summer, is in the process of refreezing. Emperor penguins are the only animals which breed in the Antarctic winter. The birds make no nests. As a matter of fact, it is the male that cares for the young ones, while the female goes out in search of food.

02 May–June

Come May or early June, it is time for the female to leave the colony in search of food. She gives the egg for incubation to the male. The male pushes the egg between its feet, under a feathered skinfold called the brood pouch. The egg stays warm and snug at 38° C, even though the temperature outside is way below 0° C.

The maintenance of temperature is very important as an exposed egg could freeze in the surrounding temperatures, killing the embryo inside. It is a tough road for the papa penguin!

03 July–August

The colony becomes quiet when the females leave in search of food. They return in July. They trudge through the snow and blizzards. The trek to the sea can be 80 km at times. The females feed themselves on foods like fish, krill, and squid.

▲ A female gentoo penguin trekking to the water

▲ The male penguin incubates the egg

▲ The male and female emperor during the mating season

01 April

Emperor penguins can be seen in thousands. It is freezing cold. The temperatures are close to 60° C with wind speeds of almost 200 kmph. But, it is time to procreate and hence time to find a mate. There is a lot of hustle and bustle in the colony as the penguins go looking for mates. They sing songs, march in an impressive manner or bow their heads together. Once they find their partner, they mate. The female produces a single egg.

In Real Life

Research has found that emperor penguins breed on ice shelves. While some breeds live on sea-ice, some are also found to live on the ice shelves. As they rely on the ice, the population of emperor penguins could rapidly decline due to global warming.

ANIMALS | BIRDS

04 July-August

By the time the females return, the male penguins are famished. They have not eaten anything for more than two months. Their only source of energy is their body fat. They have lost more than half their body weight. On the other hand, the females are big and well-fed. After their return, the female and male find each other using calls. She **regurgitates** some food and feeds the male penguin. The male gives the egg, or if it has hatched, the chick, to the female and begins its journey to the sea to find food. But at times the male is adamant on not giving the egg to the female. He has looked after it for so many months after all. The female has to really work hard to convince the male to give up the egg, so that he can go search for food.

Isn't It Amazing!

It might surprise people to learn that there are penguins in Africa! The African penguins, like the emperor penguin, have black and white feathers. These feathers keep them warm and dry in their home on the coastlines of Africa. These penguins belong to one of the smallest species.

▲ African penguins are also called 'jackass' penguins

▲ A gentoo female penguin feeding its chicks

◄ A crèche of emperor penguins

05 September

By September, the chicks grow up. They can keep themselves insulated. They need a lot more food to grow even further. The young emperor penguin needs both the parents (males are back in the colony by this time) to look for food. The parent emperor penguins leave the young in groups called 'crèches' and go hunting for food.

06 December

By December, the summer sets in the Southern Hemisphere. The ice breaks, bringing the nesting site close to the sea water. The chicks grow up into young adults. They are now capable of swimming and finding food on their own.

▲ An Adélie penguin jumping between ice floes

Knowing Birds

Did you know that there are people in the world who have dedicated their lives to learning about birds? In fact, it is an entire field of study on its own! The branch of science which deals with the study of birds is called **ornithology** and the person who studies birds is called an **ornithologist**.

Ornithology

The basic equipment any ornithologist needs is a good pair of binoculars to observe the birds. These professionals study the day-to-day lives of birds, including their feeding habits, flying techniques, mating and nesting patterns, as well as migrations. Some famous ornithologists from around the world are Allan Octavian Hume, Dr Salim Ali, Peter Scott, and Roger Tory Peterson. Read on to know some special habits and traits of birds.

Incredible Individuals

Dr Salim Ali (1896–1987) was called the 'birdman of India' because of his contributions to the field of ornithology.

The Himalayan forest thrush, which was discovered by a group of Indian and Swedish scientists, was given the scientific name *Zoothera salimalii* in honour of Dr Salim Ali.

Bird Brain

To be bird-brained means to be stupid, as birds are supposed to have small brains. Are birds really dumb though? No! Scientists have proven that birds have lots of neurons in their brains, meaning that they are intelligent. Firstly, birds migrate with an accurate sense of direction, so much so that they come back to the same homing ground they left before migration.

Studies have proven that ravens plan tasks in advance like humans; crows remember faces; parrots, especially the African grey parrot, can mimic human speech; and cockatoos, among other birds, can create music. While courting a female, a male cockatoo can create its own music by beating seed pods and twigs against tree hollows.

The Intelligent Owl

The barn owl cannot see well, but its sense of hearing is very keen. It can hear well enough to locate its prey, usually a mouse or shrew, even in thick grass. The two ears of the owl are different from each other. Its left ear can detect sounds from below, while the right can hear sounds above it. Also, the barn owl has thick and soft feathers, which make minimum noise, so the prey is not alerted.

◀ *Barn owls are amongst the most intelligent birds and have a sharp sense of hearing*

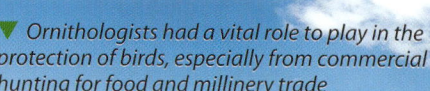

▼ *Ornithologists had a vital role to play in the protection of birds, especially from commercial hunting for food and millinery trade*

In Real Life

Birds are an important part of cultures around the world. In the *Bible*, Noah is said to have sent out a dove to see if the flood waters on Earth had receded. In India, spotting of the crow pheasant is considered a good omen, while in China the crane is a symbol of peace and longevity.

Cause and Effect

Humans do not realise it, but birds are not just things of beauty that soar in our skies. They help us in many ways. They fertilise plants, disperse seeds, help in pollination, clean up carrion, and control the populations of various insects. Today, more than 12 per cent of bird species are endangered.

In Africa, the population of eagles and vultures is dipping, while migratory birds such as the spoonbills, pelicans, and storks near the Yellow Sea are endangered. Penguins are facing a threat to their existence as the ice cover decreases in Antarctica.

▲ No sightings of Siberian cranes have been reported at Bharatpur, Rajasthan in recent years and only 3,200 remain in the world

▲ Animals and birds are losing their homes due to deforestation

Reasons for Extinction

The presence of harmful chemicals such as DDT in the atmosphere is one of the main reasons that birds face extinction. Although DDT has been banned since the 1970s (except in some malaria-prone areas of Africa), its harmful **hereditary** effects are still felt by many birds of prey in the USA. Other causes for extinction are air and marine pollution, hunting, deforestation, development in and around ecological habitats, and climate and weather changes.

International Union for Conservation of Nature

International Union for Conservation of Nature (IUCN) is an organisation established in 1948 which works towards conservation and sustainability of the environment. The IUCN Red List of Threatened Species, established in 1964, is one of the world's most reliable sources of information on global conservation of animals, plants, and fungi.

The organisation has created varied categories based on the risks faced by animals, birds, and fungi. The animals for whom the organisation has sufficient data are divided into the following categories:

- Extinct (EX)
- Extinct in Wild (EW)
- Critically Endangered (CR)
- Endangered (EN)
- Vulnerable (VU)
- Near Threatened (NT)
- Least Concern (LC)

Do Your Bit

The government will do its bit but is there something you can do to help? You can help by educating people and creating awareness about our environment. Further, we must all strive hard to protect the trees, as they are homes, not just to the birds, but to many insects and smaller animals as well. See if you can join a good conservation programme with the help of a family member.

▲ Planting trees will create more homes for birds

Word Check

Aerodynamic: It means to have qualities which make it possible to move through air easily.

Carrion: It is the decaying flesh of dead animals.

Endangered species: It refers to species where the population is so low, they could soon go extinct.

Hereditary: It refers to something that is passed from generation to generation.

Fossil: It is a bone of an animal, part of a plant, or shell whose shape has been preserved in a rock for a long period of time.

Keratin: It is a fibrous protein that is present on the outer layer of feathers, nails, and hooves.

Mating season: It is a period during which males and females of a species mate most often to produce offspring.

Moulting: It is the process by which birds shed their feathers and replace them with new feathers.

Ornithologist: It refers to a person who is involved in the study of birds.

Ornithology: It refers to the study of birds.

Piscivorous: It refers to birds that eat fish as the staple of their diets.

Ratites: It refers to a group of flightless birds like the ostrich and emu.

Regurgitate: It means to bring up the swallowed food again to the mouth. Some birds do this to feed their young ones.

Species: It refers to a group of closely related living organisms which are like each other and can interbreed to produce offspring.